In the countryside

INTRODUCTION

The countryside of the UK is amazing. From mountains to valleys, parks to farmland, and rivers and ponds to woodlands, there are many different landscapes in which you will find a vast array of insects, animals, birds, trees and plants. Miles of byways and footpaths will take you on a journey of discovery as you i-SPY the sights, sounds, smells, tastes and textures of the countryside in all its colourful glory. There are things to find and do all year round and in all weathers too, with points to collect as you go. The harder something is to find, the more points you will get, so always keep on the lookout for something new.

Here are a few tips to help you enjoy the countryside safely and respectfully:

Some plants are poisonous, so never pick and eat a plant unless you are certain it is good to eat.

Keep to footpaths when you are walking across farmland, and try not to disturb any livestock.

Always leave gates as you find them.

Take only photographs, leave only footprints.

How to use your i-SPY book

As you work through this book, you will notice that the subjects are arranged in groups or activities which are related to the seasons or kind of places where you are likely to find things. You need 1000 points to send off for your i-SPY certificate (see page 64) but that is not too difficult because there are masses of points in every book. Each entry has a star or circle and points value beside it. The stars represent harder to spot entries. As you make each i-SPY, write your score in the circle or star.

Points: 10

SOFT MOSS

There are hundreds of different types of moss. They like moisture, clean air and can grow on rocks, trees and buildings.

PRICKLY TEASEL

Points: 15

From June to October, this spiky flower head is covered with hundreds of purple flowers which attract bees and butterflies. When the flowers die, just the prickly head remains and it makes a great natural paintbrush (but watch out for the thorns on the stem).

Points: 10

FLAKY LICHEN

Lichens grow on rocks, walls and trees and are affected by the quality of the air. Many will only grow where there is clean air, whilst some prefer the nitrogen found in polluted air.

STICKY GOOSEGRASS

Points: 10

This common hedgerow plant is covered in tiny hooks that help it stick to passing animals. This helps it to spread its seeds. It also means it sticks to clothing and skin, which makes it great for sneakily sticking on people!

Points: 10

SILKY FORGET-ME-NOT PETALS

These tiny blue or purple flowers grow in clumps in spring. A German legend says when God named all of the plants, a tiny flower cried out, "Forget-me-not, oh Lord!" and that became its name. Look for them in the woods.

4

Points: 10

TICKLY FEATHER

Feathers help birds to fly and keep warm, and can protect them from water. Some birds have feathers that camouflage them so they can hide from predators, whilst others are brightly coloured or patterned to help them attract mates.

PAPERY SYCAMORE SEED

Points: 5

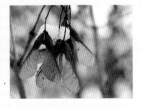

Sycamore seeds are also known as 'helicopters' because of the way they float and spin in the wind. By doing this they help the trees to spread their seeds about. This happens in the autumn.

Points: 5

WET RAINDROP

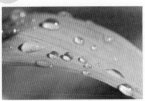

Every minute of the day around 900 million tonnes of rain falls on the earth – that's equivalent to the weight of 130 million double-decker buses!

LACY LEAF SKELETON

Points: 15

Deciduous trees like oak, beech and lime shed their leaves in autumn. These leaves provide shelter and food for all sorts of minibeasts. They gradually break down over time, usually the fleshy parts of the leaf first, leaving a 'skeleton' behind.

Points: 15

CRUMBLY SOIL FROM A MOLEHILL

Molehills are made by moles tunnelling underground, pushing up earth as they hunt for earthworms. Moles have spade-like front paws which are ideal for digging tunnels and they can tunnel up to 20m (65ft) a day!

Points: 20

HOOTING TAWNY OWL

The tawny owl is Britain's most common woodland owl (although it is not found in Ireland). The famous 't-wit t-woo' sound is actually created by two tawny owls, a female and a male, calling to each other.

CHIRPING GRASSHOPPER

Points: 10

Have you ever wandered along a grass verge or through a field in summer and heard the air buzzing with chirping grasshoppers? Grasshoppers make this noise by rubbing their hind legs against their forewings.

Points: 20

RIBBITING FROG

Some people believe frogs and toads are particularly sensitive to weather changes and that they croak louder when rain or a storm is on the way. Test this out next time you're near a pond.

RAT-A-TAT WOODPECKER

Top Spot!   Points: 35   35

You may hear male great spotted woodpeckers 'drumming' in spring, either to attract a mate or to warn off other male woodpeckers. Both males and females chisel out holes in tree trunks to make nests, or peck at the bark and look for insects with their long tongues.

Points: 30

STINKHORN FUNGUS

The stinkhorn fungus is well named! It has a slimy, olive-green cap containing its spores. The slime smells like rotting meat and attracts flies which then carry the spores away on their legs.

HONEYSUCKLE

Points: 10

This climbing plant wraps itself around other shrubs and trees. It blooms in summer, with the flowers smelling their sweetest and strongest in the evening.

WILD GARLIC

Points: 15

This plant flowers in spring and fills woodlands with its strong garlic-like scent. Wild boar like to dig up the bulbs and eat them.

Points: 15

GORSE

Gorse is actually a member of the pea family. It flowers for most of the year and its bright yellow flower heads smell strongly of coconut – just watch your nose on its sharp thorny spines!

Points: 5

BLACKBERRIES

Blackberries come from the bramble plant, ripening in late summer when they're perfect for picking. Birds, badgers, mice and butterflies are also fond of nibbling this juicy fruit.

SWEET CHESTNUTS

Points: 10

It is thought the sweet chestnut tree was brought to the UK by the Romans over 2000 years ago. The chestnuts are hidden inside a prickly case and are traditionally roasted and eaten at Christmas time. They can also be ground down into flour and used to make bread or cakes

ELDERFLOWERS

Points: 10

The elder tree flowers in early summer and the blossom is commonly used to make cordial and champagne. The flower heads can also be deep-fried to make 'fritters'.

Points: 5

ROSEHIPS

Rosehips ripen in autumn and are bursting with vitamin C. During the war people collected them to turn into syrup as other fruits were hard to get hold of. The seeds also contain tiny hairs which make a fantastic itching powder!

SPRING COLOUR

Points: 10

The UK is home to the world's best bluebell displays – they appear in spring, often growing so close together they look like a shimmering blue carpet.

Points: 10

SUMMER COLOUR

Wildflower meadows are home to lots of wildlife including butterflies, bees and grasshoppers. They usually include a colourful mix of wildflowers, such as poppies, ox-eye daisies and cornflowers.

AUTUMN COLOUR

Points: 5

The colourful autumn displays of broad-leaved trees vary depending on sunlight, rain and temperature. A bright, sunny autumn will usually lead to the most dazzling displays.

Points: 10

WINTER WHITE

A hoar frost makes everything look as if it has been coated with a layer of sparkling ice crystals. It occurs in very cold temperatures when water vapour in the air condenses on to surfaces that are below freezing, forming ice crystals.

BALANCE ON A LOG

Points: 20

Fallen branches and logs are brilliant for balancing on. As they decay, the dead wood is also a vital habitat for many creatures and fungi, providing food, shelter and a place to breed. Be careful though – they can be slippery.

SPLASH IN A MUDDY PUDDLE

It's great fun splashing about in your wellies, but animals like muddy puddles too. Swallows sometimes use mud from puddles to build their nests and some species of butterflies drink from muddy puddles to get extra salts and minerals that they can't get from nectar.

WEAVE IN AND OUT OF TREES

Points: 10

Planting trees either side of paths or roads has been very popular for hundreds of years. Clumber Park in Nottinghamshire has the longest double-planted lime avenue in Europe – 3.2km (2 miles) long and made up of 1296 trees, all around 170 years old.

Points: 5

KICK THROUGH LEAVES

Watch out for dazzling displays in autumn as the leaves on deciduous trees turn yellow, orange and gold before falling to the ground. The colours vary depending on how warm and dry the summer and autumn weather is.

Points: 15

HUG A HUGE, OLD TREE

The older a tree gets, the bigger its trunk is, but the size varies a lot depending on the type of tree it is. Sweet chestnut, yew, oak and lime are among the biggest and some of them have been growing for hundreds or even thousands of years.

CRAWL THROUGH LONG GRASS

Points: 10

Patches of long grass are great places to look for minibeasts. You can encourage bugs in your garden by leaving a corner to go 'wild' – if you stop cutting the grass and create a wood pile you might attract frogs, toads and hedgehogs too.

Points: 15

HIDE BEHIND OR IN A HUGE TREE

Trees are fantastic for hide and seek. As they grow older some become hollow, like the Bowthorpe Oak in Lincolnshire which can fit 39 people inside! Can you find a hollow tree to hide in?

FIND A FACE IN THE TREES

Points: 20

Take a closer look at the trees around you, can you see any faces looking back? Knobbly growths, gnarled roots and dark animal tunnels underneath trees often look like eyes, noses and mouths.

Points: 15

CLIMB A TREE

The best trees for climbing are big ones like oak, beech and ash. Look for healthy looking ones with plenty of strong branches at regular intervals. A good tip is to climb near the trunk, where the branches are strongest, but take care not to fall off!

BUILD A DEN

Top Spot!   Points: 35

Can you find a secret shelter hidden in the woods? Make your own with fallen branches, grass and leaves. What can you find to make it waterproof and windproof?

CENTIPEDE

Points: 10

Centipedes don't actually have 100 legs, it's usually only between 30–40. You can tell them apart from millipedes because centipedes only have one pair of legs on each segment of their body, whereas millipedes have two pairs. This makes centipedes better adapted for running. Centipedes have poisonous claws which they use to attack and capture prey.

Points: 25

GREEN SHIELD BUG

The green shield bug gets its name from the colour and shape of its body. It is also sometimes called a 'green stink bug' because it gives out a terrible smell if handled or disturbed. Green shield bugs turn brown just before they hibernate for winter, then they turn back to green when they wake up in spring.

Points: 5

SNAIL

Snails are one of the slowest moving species on earth. The garden snail is the fastest type of snail, with a top speed of around 50 metres (164 feet) per hour. Snails are also extremely strong and can lift up to 10 times their own body weight.

EARTHWORM

Points: 5

Earthworms help to recycle decaying plant matter by eating it and turning it into fertile soil. By loosening and mixing up the soil they also help to bring nutrients closer to the surface.

Points: 15

LACEWING

Lacewings get their name from the delicate network of veins in their transparent wings, which look like lace. Both adults and larvae are carnivorous – the larvae suck the juice from aphids, then hide under the drained bodies to creep up on unsuspecting prey!

Points: 10

SEVEN-SPOT LADYBIRD

Ladybirds are brightly coloured to warn predators they don't taste very nice. They can also release drops of strong-smelling, yellow liquid to warn off potential predators. Both adult ladybirds and the larvae eat aphids, a big pest in gardens, so ladybirds are a great friend to gardeners.

ANT

Points: 10

Ants are very strong and can lift up to 50 times their own body weight. This is because ants have a different muscle structure to humans – if you had the same muscle structure as an ant you would be able to lift a car above your head!

Points: 25

SPECKLED WOOD BUTTERFLY

You'll find this butterfly in woods, gardens and hedgerows. The adults rarely drink nectar from flowers, preferring instead to feed on honeydew secreted by aphids. Male speckled wood butterflies are particularly territorial so you'll often see them circling up into the air and clashing wings in battle.

WOODLOUSE

Points: 5

Woodlice belong to the crustacean family and are more closely related to crabs and shrimps than to other insects. You'll find them in damp, dark places like under rocks and logs, as well as in compost heaps.

Points: 25

FIVE-SPOT BURNET MOTH

The five-spot burnet moth is one of the few moths that fly during the day. It is very distinctive with black wings and five red spots on each wing. The bright colouring acts as a warning to potential predators that the moth tastes awful.

WATER BOATMAN

Points: 15 15

Water boatmen are commonly found in ponds, lakes and slow-moving rivers. They use their long back legs like oars to propel themselves through the water, so they look a bit like tiny rowing boats! They have a special technique which lets them stay under the water – they collect air at the surface and carry it with them as a bubble which allows them to breathe underwater.

15 **Points: 15**

POND SKATER

Pond skaters use surface tension to literally walk on water! The tiny hairs on their feet repel the water and allow them to skate across the surface. These hairs also help them find their prey – they sense vibrations and ripples on the water's surface, helping the pond skater to detect insects which have fallen in.

Points: 20

FROGSPAWN

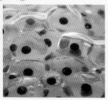

The black balls are the eggs which are surrounded by a protective jelly that stops them drying out. A female frog can lay up to 2000 eggs, but only about five of these will grow up into adult frogs – late frosts can kill frogspawn and many of the eggs get eaten by predators.

TOADSPAWN

Points: 30

Toad spawn is easily recognised because it forms long strings of eggs, a bit like a necklace, unlike frogspawn which looks like a mass of jelly.

Points: 20

TADPOLES

Frogspawn and toadspawn develop into tadpoles, which in turn start to grow legs and become froglets. When tadpoles start growing their legs they become carnivorous and if there isn't enough food around they may start to eat each other!

LESSER CELANDINE

Points: 15

This is one of the first flowers to appear at the end of winter, brightening up forest floors with a carpet of yellow 'stars' between February and May. It has narrow, pointed petals which close up before rain and at night-time. It also has dark green, heart-shaped leaves.

Points: 15

ASH

The ash tree's flowers look a bit like purple brains, or coral, exploding out of the black buds! They appear in April, before the leaves appear – the ash tree is one of the UK's last native trees to come into leaf.

WOOD SORREL

Points: 15

Wood sorrel mostly grows in woodlands and hedgerows. The white, pink-tinged flowers are very delicate and fold themselves up during rain and at night to protect the pollen inside. This is thought to be why it is sometimes known as 'sleeping beauty'.

Points: 15

WOOD ANEMONE

The wood anemone is one of the first spring flowers to appear on the woodland floor, forming a carpet of dazzling white flowers from March to May. Wood anemone spreads very slowly, so it's often a sign of an ancient woodland. If you find it in a meadow or hedgerow, it might indicate a forest used to be there many years ago – for this reason the flower is sometimes known as a 'woodland ghost'.

EARLY PURPLE ORCHID

Points: 20

This flower mostly grows in woodlands. In folklore, the early purple orchid is associated with love, and was often used in love potions. The flowers are a vivid pink/purple colour and the leaves are green with dark purple/black spots on them.

BIRD'S-FOOT TREFOIL

Points: 15

This plant is often known as 'bacon and eggs' because of the yellow, red and orange colours of the flowers. It is mostly found in grassland areas and blooms between April and September.

Points: 15

BUGLE

This plant was thought to be a cure-all by Medieval herbalists, who thought it helped to heal everything from broken bones to ulcers! It flowers between April and July and grows in damp grasslands and woodland clearings.

WOOD AVENS

Points: 15

This plant is widespread and grows in woods and hedgerows. According to folklore it was one of the most powerful charms against evil spirits. Plants hung over the door were believed to be able to stop the devil entering the house!

Points: 10

DANDELION

After a dandelion has flowered, it produces a round seedhead known as a 'clock'. These contain up to 200 seeds, each one shaped a little like a parachute, which helps them blow away in the wind. The sap inside a dandelion stem makes a great invisible ink – perfect for writing secret messages!

FOXGLOVE

Points: 15

Foxgloves produce between 20–80 flowers on each stem, with each flowerhead lasting about a week. The plant is poisonous, as indicated by one of its common names, 'dead man's bells'. Despite being toxic the foxglove is also the source of an important drug, Digitalin, which is used in very small doses to treat heart disease.

Watch out for adult birds flying to and from nests, bringing food for their young. Most birds bring back insects and worms to feed their babies, but some seed-eating birds also regurgitate seed to help the youngsters' digestion.

Points: 25

The name comes from the 'eyes' on the wings, which look similar to those on a peacock's tail and help to scare off predators such as birds. Peacock butterflies like to feast on nectar from thistles and buddleia, as well as rotting fruit in autumn!

Points: 15

Red-tailed bumblebees usually nest underground, but you'll often see them buzzing around gardens and grasslands that are rich in clover, drinking the sweet nectar.

Points: 25

These bright turquoise and orange birds perch next to slow-moving or still water, looking for food. When the right moment comes along they swiftly dive into the water, catching a fish with their long beaks. They also eat aquatic insects.

OAK

Points: 10

The English oak is one of Britain's most well known and most loved trees. It doesn't reach its full height until it's at least 150 years old and can live for 1000 years or more.

Points: 20

LIME

Lime trees have distinctive heart-shaped leaves. The common lime was planted so often in towns and parks in the 17th century that it gained the name 'common' as a result.

Points: 15

HAZEL

Hazel branches are really flexible, especially in spring when green branches can even be tied into a knot!

FIELD MAPLE

Points: 10

Field maple seeds are also known as 'helicopter' seeds and are shaped so they spin as they fall, this helps carry the seeds as far as possible in the wind, allowing new trees to grow in other locations.

Points: 10

BEECH

Few flowers can grow in beech woods during the summer because of the deep shade cast by the trees and the thick carpet of fallen leaves.

HORSE CHESTNUT

Points: 10

The world conker championships have been held in Northamptonshire every year since 1965. The name 'horse chestnut' supposedly comes from the practice of feeding conkers to horses to cure them of illness.

Points: 10

ROWAN

The rowan tree is steeped in history and mythology – rowan timber was used by Druids to make staffs and magic wands due to its straightness. It was also traditionally used for tool handles, cartwheels and beams as it's very strong.

HAWTHORN

Points: 10

Keep an eye out for the hawthorn's white blossom in late spring – when it appears it is a good sign that summer is on the way. It is also said that hawthorn flowers smell like rotten flesh. Give them a sniff, what do you think they smell like?

Points: 15

HOLLY

The tradition of decorating the house with holly during winter goes back thousands of years. The fruits tend to ripen in winter but the evergreen nature of the plant means that its glossy, richly green leaves are on show throughout the summer too.

Points: 35   Top Spot!

SILVER BIRCH

With its slender trunk, silver bark and fluttering leaves, the silver birch is often called the 'lady of the woods'. You'll often see the spotty red toadstool, fly agaric, growing at the base of silver birch and feeding on the tree's roots, in autumn.

WHITE POPLAR

Points: 25

The bark of a white poplar tree has very distinctive diamond-shaped markings, called lenticels, which help to identify it all year round.

Points: 20

SWEET CHESTNUT

Older sweet chestnuts are very recognisable because the bark develops swirly ridges, which spiral up the tree a bit like a helter-skelter. They are also usually magnificent in size, with many having huge hollow trunks that several people can fit into at once!

You will find fungi and mushrooms in most wooded areas. They are great to look at but can be very poisonous so please don't touch any or you could get very ill.

FLY AGARIC

Points: 25

This poisonous toadstool, which often appears in fairytales and stories, mostly grows at the base of birch trees. The red cap is covered in white spots, which are sometimes washed off by the rain.

Points: 40   **Top Spot!**

CHICKEN OF THE WOODS

This is a bracket fungus growing in shelf-like layers. It is commonly found from late spring through to autumn, often on oak trees where it causes rot which can result in hollowing.

Points: 25

CHANTERELLE

This funnel-shaped fungus grows in woodlands, often growing in the same spot year after year. It's the colour of apricots and smells a bit like them too!

JELLY EAR

Points: 30

This fungus grows on dead trees, mostly elder, and looks like rubbery brown ears. It shrinks down to hard, dark lumps in dry weather – then transforms back to 'ears' when it rains.

Points: 30

PINK WAXCAP

The pink waxcap is also known as the ballerina – as it gets older the pink cap flattens and splits, with the edges often flicking up like a tutu. Look for it in areas of short grass.

Points: 35   **Top Spot!**

GIANT PUFFBALL

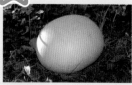

These huge mushrooms can grow bigger than a person's head and contain up to 7 trillion spores. They grow in grassy areas – often in rings – and burst once they mature, releasing the spores in a dusty cloud.

KING ALFRED'S CAKES

Top Spot!   **Points: 40**

Insects and other small animals often make their home in this fungus. As it grows old it gets a hard, shiny, black crust like burnt buns and can be used for lighting fires as it burns like charcoal.

Points: 35   **Top Spot!**

SHAGGY INKCAP

This fungus has amazing strength and can even push its way through tarmac! It drips black ink from the edges of its cap – ink made from this mushroom was used to sign the Magna Carta in 1215.

Points: 30

YELLOW BRAIN

This grows on dead branches and is parasitic, meaning it feeds off other fungi. Its bright yellow colour makes it easy to spot after wet weather, where it looks like yellow brains spilling out!

ORANGE PEEL FUNGUS

Top Spot! **Points: 35**

This fungus belongs to the 'cup' family and grows on damp bare soil and grass. It has fragile, thin flesh which splits easily so it looks like discarded orange peel.

ACORN

Points: 10

An oak tree doesn't usually produce a large amount of acorns until it reaches 40–50 years old. The number of acorns changes each year, but every three to five years they will produce a bumper crop of up to 50,000 acorns! This is known as a mast year.

Points: 10

The Romans used elderberry juice as hair dye! Elder branches also make fantastic pea shooters – they are light and filled with pith, which can be easily hollowed out.

ROWAN BERRY

Points: 10

Rowan berries can be made into jams and jellies, but they are very bitter when eaten raw. They are packed with vitamin C and are a great winter food for birds, especially redwings and blackbirds.

Points: 10

CONKERS

Conkers is a game traditionally played in playgrounds. You search for a really hard conker with no cracks, then attach it to the end of a piece of string and hit it against your opponent's conker, battling to see whose conker is the hardest.

ASH KEY

Points: 10

The ash tree can grow up to 30 metres (98ft) in height. It grows clusters of 'keys' or winged seeds in autumn, which are swept away by the wind. The wood from ash trees is very strong and flexible, so it is often used to make furniture, tool handles, even hockey sticks.

Points: 15

HAZELNUTS

Hazelnuts are eaten by both people and animals. Squirrels and mice help hazel to spread by collecting the nuts, burying them, then forgetting about them so they grow into trees.

BLACKTHORN

Points: 15

The fruits of the blackthorn are called sloes and although they aren't poisonous they are extremely sour. Cooked sloes can be used to make jams, jellies and wine.

Points: 10

HAWTHORN

Hawthorn is a very common hedgerow shrub. The berries are known as haws and are eaten by many birds and mammals. Lots of animals also make their homes or nests within hawthorn hedges.

The hedgehog's diet of pests like slugs and snails makes it a popular visitor with gardeners. It also eats beetles and earthworms, feasting throughout early autumn to store up enough energy to hibernate through winter. You're most likely to see a hedgehog after dark.

Points: 30

STAG

During autumn, the 'rutting' or mating season starts. Stags pursue groups of female deer, bellowing loudly to drive away other males that might be interested. Sometimes stags will fight each other, clashing their antlers together in a battle to see who is superior.

BAT

Top Spot! **Points: 35**

Bats are the only mammals that can fly. They are nocturnal, so they mostly sleep during the day and come out at night. All UK bats eat insects – the common pipistrelle can eat as many as 3000 in one night!

Points: 25

FOX

Fox coats look their best in autumn, when the adults' fur has grown back after the summer moult. Foxes are scavengers and eat almost anything – from birds to insects, small mammals to autumn berries, and even scraps from dustbins. They are often seen in towns and cities.

Points: 5

The full moon is a lunar phase occurring when the moon is on the opposite side of the earth from the sun, and all three bodies are aligned in a straight line. It appears as an entire circle in the sky. The only month that can occur without a full moon is February.

SPIDER'S WEB

Points: 10

Spiders produce super strong, flexible silk to spin webs and catch prey. When an insect gets trapped in the sticky web and struggles, the spider is alerted by vibrations travelling along the silky threads. The spider then wraps their prey up in silk before eating them.

TREE SILHOUETTE

Points: 10

Look out for dead trees standing out amongst their leafy neighbours. These standing dead trees, known as 'snags', are important sources of food and shelter to a wide range of wildlife including fungi, insects, bats and birds.

Points: 5

CROW

The crow is one of our most intelligent birds. They tend to prefer their own company to being part of a group, so look out for them on their own. They eat almost anything, including insects, seeds, fruits and dead animals.

Points: 15

Mist is made up of lots of tiny water droplets suspended in the air. It is very similar to fog, in fact the difference between the two types depends on how dense they are and how this affects visibility – fog is denser with less visibility, mist is less dense with more visibility.

Starlings flock together in an attempt to make themselves safe from predators. This flocking is called a 'murmuration' and often involves thousands of birds swooping and soaring together. So many starlings roosted on the hands of London's Big Ben in 1949 that they stopped the famous clock!

SPIDER

Points: 5

In early autumn male spiders start scurrying around looking for a mate, so this is why you might suddenly notice more around your house at this time of year. They much prefer living outdoors though, so if you find one carefully capture it and put it back outside.

Points: 20

COMPLETE SILENCE

Try and find somewhere you can sit in silence for a couple of minutes – it's tricky, you'll probably still be able to hear birdsong, insects or a whisper of wind. In fact the only place there is true silence is outer space – this is because it's a vacuum, where sounds cannot travel.

SNOWFLAKE

Points: 15

Snowflakes form up in the clouds and their intricate shapes vary depending on how high they form, as well as the temperature, humidity and dust in the air. See how many snowflakes you can catch next time it snows. How quickly do they melt?

Points: 20

ICICLES

Icicles form when water drips from an object and freezes because the air temperature is below zero degrees Celsius. Look out for icicles hanging from tree branches in cold, frosty woods.

FROZEN PUDDLE

Points: 10

Spare a thought for thirsty birds when the weather is very cold – as streams, puddles and ponds freeze over birds lose vital sources of water for drinking and bathing. You can help by putting a bird bath in your garden, keeping it topped up with fresh, clean water and breaking any ice that forms.

Points: 15

FRESH SNOW

Freshly fallen snow is brilliant for playing in! As snow falls, it gets blown about by the wind which can cause snow drifts, as well as the 'spray-on' effect like the beech tree trunks.

Points: 40   Top Spot!

BADGER

A badger print is similar to a dog's paw print, but you can tell them apart because a badger has five toes and a sausage-shaped pad at the back.

Points: 35 **Top Spot!**

DEER

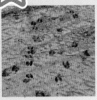

Deer are 'ungulates', which means they have split hooves. They leave distinctive 'two-toed' prints in mud and snow. They also have long legs with powerful muscles which help them to run fast and jump.

SQUIRREL

Points: 25

Squirrels don't hibernate in winter because they can't store enough energy to sleep for such a long period. Instead they build a large drey to cosy up in and only venture out to find nuts and other items they buried in autumn. They leave complicated tracks – a mixture of claws and pads.

Points: 5

WELLIES

Wellies get their name from the first Duke of Wellington, who had his shoemaker design a comfortable, hard-wearing style of boot. Today they are waterproof and usually made from rubber. The bumps and grooves on the soles are called the tread – see how many different patterns you can spot.

ASH

Ash twigs are grey with large, velvety-black pointy buds. Did you know the ash tree belongs to the olive family?

 Points: 10

BEECH

Beech twigs often grow in a zig-zag shape, with long, brown torpedo-shaped buds at alternate points. Beech trees produce dense foliage, which falls to the ground in autumn creating a thick carpet of leaves.

HORSE CHESTNUT

Points: 10

In winter, the ends of horse chestnut twigs have small sticky buds on them. Look out for horseshoe-shaped marks on the twigs, left by the previous year's leaves.

Points: 10

FIELD MAPLE

The field maple is the only maple tree that is native to the UK. It is also the only maple whose leaves do not turn orange or red in autumn – instead they change to a golden yellow. Buds grow in pairs on opposite sides of the twigs.

MOUNTAIN

Points: 20

Britain's highest peaks are in Scotland, north Wales and the Lake District, though there are also many smaller mountains and hills across the rest of the country. Some were made by volcanoes millions of years ago.

Points: 10

WOODLAND

Woods are a great place to go for a walk. See how many different types of tree you can spot while you're there, and look out for woodland creatures too.

Points: 10

Starting off as streams in the hills, rivers flow downhill and increase in volume as they go. They usually flow into the sea, a lake or another river. By this time they can be really wide and slow-moving.

CAVE

Points: 25

On rocky coasts the waves pound the cliffs to create caves. Inland caves are formed when water dissolves rock as it trickles through cracks. Some cave systems go on for miles and have huge caverns.

Points: 15

BEACH

Beaches can be sandy or stony but are always great places to play. Try building a sandcastle, jumping over the waves or throwing stones into the sea.

WETLAND

Points: 20

Where low-lying land becomes waterlogged for all or part of the year, wetlands are created which are an important habitat for plants and birds. On the coast, saltwater marshes attract different species.

INDEX

How to get your i-SPY certificate and badge

Let us know when you've become a Super-spotter with 1000 points and we'll send you a special certificate and badge!

HERE'S WHAT TO DO!

✅ Ask an adult to check your score.

✅ Visit www.collins.co.uk/i-SPY to apply for your certificate. If you are under the age of 13 you will need a parent or guardian to do this.

✅ We'll send your certificate via email and you'll receive a brilliant badge through the post!